Give Us & Forgive Us

Neil C. Ellis

WORD & SPIRIT
PUBLISHING

All Scripture quotations unless otherwise designated are taken from the New King James Version® NKJV. Copyright © 1982 by Thomas Nelson. Used by permission. All rights reserved.

Scripture quotations marked King James Version (KJV) are public domain, and may be freely used.

Scriptures taken from the Holy Bible, New International Version®, NIV®. Copyright © 1973, 1978, 1984, 2011 by Biblica, Inc.™ Used by permission of Zondervan. All rights reserved worldwide. www.zondervan.com The "NIV" and "New International Version" are trademarks registered in the United States Patent and Trademark Office by Biblica, Inc.™

Give Us & Forgive Us
© 2020 by Neil C. Ellis
ISBN: 978-1-949106-51-0

Published by Word and Spirit Publishing
P.O. Box 701403
Tulsa, Oklahoma 74170
wordandspiritpublishing.com

Printed in the United States of America. All rights reserved under International Copyright Law. Content and/or cover may not be reproduced in whole or in part in any form without the expressed written consent of the Publisher.

Contents

Introduction v
Books 1 and 2 Recap 1
Give Us This Day Our Daily Bread.......9
Forgive Us as We Forgive Others........39

Introduction

IN THIS BOOK, WE WILL NAVIGATE SOME of the most crucial topics of prayer that every believer needs to understand in order to make it in this world: provision and forgiveness.

"Give us this day our daily bread": **This is a petition for provision.**

"Forgive us our trespasses, as we forgive those who trespass against us": **This is a petition for pardon.**

If you have lived for any length of time on this earth, then you know, as many learned before you, we all need a lot of help and a lot of grace in life. Growing up in the natural is a process of becoming more and more independent. At first, as infants and young children, we rely on our parents for everything. We need their help to dress us, train us, drive us places, feed us, and teach us how to handle life. As we get older, we learn how to dress ourselves, drive ourselves around, take care of our own problems, and pay for our own food and shelter. This is the way life is supposed to be for us, for independence is a sign of maturity.

However, like many things in the supernatural realm, God has it set up completely opposite from the way things work in the natural. The more mature you become, spiritually speaking, the more *dependent* you become! You begin to rely more and more on God instead of yourself. To the world, you will look incredibly independent, because you will be well taken care of without depending on anyone or anything else, but you know that, in reality, you wholly and completely depend upon your Father. When it comes to making a petition for provision and a petition for forgiveness, you are firmly placing yourself under God, dependent upon Him for His supply and His approval. You want your life to be pleasing in His eyes, and for

INTRODUCTION

your increase to come from Him instead of from yourself. If you have a desire to walk completely free of burdens, full of provision and purpose, then you will be greatly rewarded in discovering the power that is found when praying under these two headings in the model prayer. Let's begin!

Books 1 and 2 Recap

Books 1 and 2 Recap

EACH BOOK IN THIS SERIES PROVIDES teaching on what many call the "Lord's Prayer." This is really a misnomer because forgiveness is asked for in the prayer, and we know Jesus never sinned. Therefore, He had no need to ask for forgiveness. So, Jesus was really giving an example, an outline, a model for us to pattern our own prayers after. This prayer could be more accurately referred to as the "Model Prayer." Within the framework of the outline, there are different headings, including:

- *"Our Father" (heading number 1)*
- *"Who art in heaven" (heading number 2)*
- *"Hallowed be Thy name" (heading number 3)*

This prayer was never meant to just be recited verbatim. The headings simply provide the structure in the outline, a formula for how to shape your own prayers. So, when you say, "Our Father, who art in heaven, hallowed be Thy name," you have only uttered a list of headings. But, based on your knowledge of the Scripture, based on your relationship with God, based on your individual situations, and based upon your particular need at the time, you can determine how to fill the gaps in with more details after every heading.

This model prayer is an outline, and an outline can be expanded or condensed as much or as little as you wish. In other words, this model can be used for a three-to-five-minute prayer, or it can be used for a ten-to-fifteen-minute prayer. The same model can be used for a thirty-minute prayer, a forty-five-minute prayer, or a fifty-minute prayer—and it's the same model that those of us who know about tarrying before God use in our longer prayers. The same model can be used for an hour, two hours, or three hours of prayer.

For however long you decide or feel led to pray, when you stick to this model, you will cover every area of your life with the Lord.

Between the moments you said the words "our" and "amen," there'll not be any need or any issue in your life that you will not have touched.

The structure in this prayer model has a flow to it, and you must go with that flow. The headings in the outline are divided into three major categories.

> Category one is all about God: "Our *Father*, hallowed be *Thy* name. *Thy* Kingdom come. *Thy* will be done."

> Category two is all about us: "Give *us* this day *our* daily bread. Forgive *us* as *we* forgive others. Lead *us* not into temptation. Deliver *us* from evil."

> Category three takes us back to God again: "For *Thine* is the

kingdom, the power, and the glory forever and ever. Amen."

Clearly, the intent is for the model prayer to begin with God and to end with God. Some theologians call this a "sandwich structure"—God is in the two ends, and we are in the middle.

In the first book, we discovered what the first three headings were all about. For the first heading, "Our Father," we learned that we are not an only child, and that we have a loving Father. For the second heading, we are put into remembrance of His position over us. We are reminded that His ways and His thoughts are far above ours, and that He has an excellent vantage point to see what is coming down the road for us. So even when circumstances catch *us* by surprise, they are no surprise to *God*. For the third heading, we are told to give honor and glory to God's name. We considered many of the names listed in God's Word and observed how each of those names gives us insight into His nature.

In the second book, we discussed the next few headings: "Thy kingdom come, Thy will be done on earth as it is in heaven." For the heading "Thy kingdom come," we learned that *kingdom* is simply two words put together: a *king's domain*. So, when we pray for God's kingdom to come, we are praying for His rule and reign to come into our lives. We also considered the heading "Thy will be done on earth as it is in heaven." We discovered the differences between the decreed, or sovereign, will of God; the perceptive will of God; the preferential will of God; and the discerned will of God. And we also saw how essential it is to know the will of God which leads to the strengthening of our faith. We cannot believe God will do something unless we first find out if He said He would do it.

If you have not yet read Books 1 and 2, it is essential reading that will bless you greatly. Now let's dive into our part in the sandwich structure of the model prayer!

Give Us
This Day
Our Daily Bread

Give Us This Day Our Daily Bread

In this manner, therefore, pray:
Our Father in heaven,
Hallowed be Your name.
Your kingdom come.
Your will be done
On earth as it is in heaven.
Give us this day our daily bread.

—Matthew 6:9–11

So many people are afraid to talk about the topic of provision. They are worried they'll be labeled "materialistic" or "unspiritual" if they talk about provision. Yet Jesus, when teaching His disciples to pray, in the first heading that involves *us, His people,* asked God for provision. He is leading the charge in this section with a request for material help! The last thing you should ever be afraid to do is follow Jesus' example! And what would it say about God if His children were always hungry, poor, and begging for bread? What a poor witness!

God wants you to be well provided for, with plenty left over with which you can bless others. When people look at the life of a believer, they should want to be like that person! When they see us walk in the peace that is beyond comprehension, with a joy that fuels everything we do, and a provision that we aren't smart enough to obtain on our own—they will want what we have!

Many people get so hung up when it comes to the topic of provision. The Bible may seem like it contradicts itself, especially when you consider what God said to Adam after the fall:

"In the sweat of your face you shall eat bread till you return to the ground, for out of it you were

taken; for dust you are, and to dust you shall return."

—GENESIS 3:19

And then you read how Jesus said to His disciples, "When you pray, pray these words: **'Give us this day our daily bread.'**" That raises the question for many: *"So, should we earn our bread, or should we ask for our bread?"*

Two chapters before Jesus taught His disciples this model prayer, He said this: *"Man shall not live by bread alone, but by every word that proceeds from the mouth of God"* (Matthew 4:4).

The same Jesus said both of these things. Jesus was acting on God's behalf on this earth, which means that if Jesus said it, then it is as if God the Father has said it. So, what is God trying to tell us?

Even Paul, by the direction of the Holy Spirit, wrote in one of his letters to the church at Thessalonica: *"For even when we were with you, we commanded you this: If anyone will not work, neither shall he eat"* (2 Thessalonians 3:10).

I submit to you that none of these verses contradict or conflict with one another. If anything, these verses complement one another! If you are wondering where you end and where God begins when it comes to your provision, then you are reading the right book. These words will unveil the truth behind receiving God's provision for your life through prayer.

When we pray, "Give us this day our daily bread," we are confessing our dependence upon God to meet our needs in this world on a daily basis. Notice the word *"daily."* Some people have misconstrued the meaning of this word in this prayer. They have labeled this to mean, "God, give me just enough provision to make it through the day…" But this is the furthest thing from the truth! God is **El Shaddai**! He is the God of **more than enough**! God only giving us enough to scrape through the day—that conflicts with everything we know about God. *This word "daily" in the model prayer* *doesn't refer to a set amount of provision, but rather the consistency of time spent with the Father.*

The word *daily* insinuates that we should be in prayer daily. God's provision comes through our daily connection with Him. It is through prayer that we connect with God. It is through that connection that God is able to cause resources to flow to you. He is able to give you daily provision, or your "daily bread" because you are linked to the Source of your provision! Do you see the difference? So, to have this daily provision, we must have a daily prayer life. As saved as we may be, developing a prayer life is not automatic. It requires us to be intentional and sincere. We must set aside time to pray, and then safeguard our time with the Lord. We must prioritize our relationship with the Lord above everything else in our lives.

There may be days when you feel like He is far from you, and that your prayers are just bouncing off the walls, not going anywhere. Satan will try to convince you of this too! He sure doesn't want you to develop a strong prayer life! The devil is afraid of any man, woman, or child who establishes a solid connection to God through prayer, because from that point on, if he messes with you, he is messing with God.

However, like every aspect of the believer's life, it requires faith to override the feelings you experience and pray with assurance that your Father hears you. There will be days when you feel alone, and days when it feels as if God is right there in the room with you. But to have a strong prayer life is not to equate the effectiveness of your prayer by the feelings you get when you pray. Rather, you must base the strength of your prayer life on the validity of your requests through the Word of God. It can be a battle to start out, to develop a value for prayer, and to spend the time you need to spend with your Father. But it is worth it!

Yes, prayer is essential for you to accomplish your purpose. Yes, prayer will provide you with daily provision. But more than that, on a personal note, as children of God, we have one of the greatest privileges that salvation has provided to us, the ability to have a real relationship with our Creator and heavenly Father. This is a relationship you'll be able to enjoy both on this earth and in heaven. Whenever you die on this earth and move to heaven, you'll be talking to the same God that you have been speaking to your whole life. So, don't be a stranger! Start your relationship with Him now!

The second thing to keep in mind when praying under this heading of *daily provision* is this:

No matter what the need is, that need is never greater than who God is.

Your need takes second place to the personhood of God. That should give you hope regardless of how dire your situation may be. It is amazing how big something can look when it is right in front of your face. If you were to put your hand right next to your face, it would look bigger than a skyscraper that is in the distance. This is the power of perspective. Satan's goal is to make the problems in your life take up your full view, blocking your vision. The problems can look so massive to you that it seems like you'll never be able to escape or overcome them. This is why Jesus instructs you to begin your prayer by focusing on *God* instead of *yourself*. This way, the moment you begin to ask God for help, you are already aware of just how big and loving He is!

So often, the reason some of us don't ask for provision from our Father is because we think it's something God wouldn't want us to request from Him. There is nothing in your life—no area of your life—that God is not concerned about. Praying this phrase, "Give us this day our daily bread," is not your idea. It is God's idea. There is no need to feel guilty when you ask for daily provision. You didn't put this instruction in the Bible. Jesus did. And when Jesus directs us to follow this prayer model, and we ask God for provision in accordance with His instruction, then we are actually acting in obedience instead of selfishness! When we pray, "Give us this day our daily bread," we are obeying Jesus' instruction to ask our Father for the things that we need to make it through each and every day. You are not enlisting some special, self-seeking prayer request by bringing up your need for provision; you are obeying God! Remember, Jesus said, "When you pray, do it like this…." and then He said to pray these words: "Give us this day our daily bread."

The instruction to pray, "Give us this day our daily bread," is more than just a prayer request. When properly understood, it describes an entirely different way of looking at life.

Give us this day our daily bread.

Do not take these seven words casually; these seven words can change your life completely if, when you pray them, you have an understanding of what it is that you're asking of God.

In this one petition that we make of our heavenly Father, we have identified the *who*, the *what*, and the *when*. "Give us"—that's who. "This day"—that's when. And "our daily bread"—that's what we are asking for. So, this petition opens us up to a whole new way of thinking and a whole new way of life. I call it ***"daily bread living."***

Daily bread living is all about three important things. Number one, daily bread living includes learning to express gratitude to God for all of His many blessings. Number two, daily bread living involves learning to live in the confidence that God will meet your needs every day. And number three, daily bread living means living with generosity toward those who are less fortunate than you. That's daily bread living.

If you pray this prayer enough with a clear understanding, it will open you up to a whole new way of looking at life, and push you into this, what I call "daily bread living." If this prayer is ever going to become a meaningful and significant part of your reality, it must first affect the way you live your life. James 4:2 also speaks of the antithesis of daily bread living:

> *You lust and do not have. You murder and covet and cannot obtain. You fight and war.* **Yet you do not have because you do not ask.**
>
> —JAMES 4:2, emphasis mine

The problem here is not that you desire something. The problem here is not that you have a goal to obtain something. The problem here is the method you employ to obtain that thing. Are you trying to obtain something on your own merits? Are you so strong-willed and intelligent that you believe you can gain the whole world on your own? And will it ever be enough? Is it worth your soul?

There is no need to lust after what other people have. You will not receive anything by doing that. There is no need to fight. A war will only deplete you, not add to you. The reason you have not is because you ask not. You don't have to envy other people or copy the world's method of how to acquire things! Besides, the plans God has for your brothers and sisters are different from the plans He has for you.

Just because you see God do something for your friends or one of your relatives, this does not mean He's going to do that same thing for you. It may not be in your plan. You cannot get mad at other people based on what God is doing with them and not with you.

There are things you may do that prevent you from receiving these things as well. For example, God says that He resists the proud but promotes the humble. So, if you've got a spirit of arrogance and pride in your life, there are some things God's going to withdraw from you until He feels He can trust you with them without losing you as His child.

God's main reason for creating us is to have fellowship with Him. If He feels that your attitude or your character has not developed to the place that you can handle a major situation without it affecting your relationship with Him, then He will always opt to protect that relationship. You have got to trust God! He is smarter than you. If He says you are ready when you do not feel ready, then you are ready. If He says you are not ready even though you feel ready, then you are not ready. This seems like a no-brainer, but we all need to be reminded of some obvious things from time to time.

Whatever plans God has for your life *will* come to pass if you maintain a pure heart of love toward God and other people. Then, when you pray, by the time you finish, you shouldn't have one jealous bone in your body. You just talked to the Creator of the universe, who is also your Provider and your Father. Coincidentally,

He also loves you very much. If you really believe that, then it will cause you to express gratitude to God for all of His blessings, to live in confidence that God will meet your needs every day, and to overflow with generosity toward those who are less fortunate than you. In short, you'll initiate "daily bread living" in your life.

> *"For I know the plans I have for you," declares the L*ORD*, "plans to prosper you and not to harm you, plans to give you hope and a future."*
>
> —JEREMIAH 29:11 NIV

According to Jeremiah 29:11, we should not worry about the plans God has for us! The plans God has for us do not include evil. The plans He has for us are custom-made for us. They can't fit anybody else's life.

So, let's break down these seven words even further. Let's look at the first word, *give*. "**Give** us this day our daily bread." Notice that Jesus does not ask us to ask the Father to sell us anything, or lend us anything, or trust us with anything. No, no, Jesus said, "When you pray, ask the Lord to *give* to you." He sums this up later on in one of the other gospels when He says, "Do not fear, little flock, for it is your Father's good pleasure to give you the kingdom" (Luke 12:32). He *wants* to give you the whole kingdom. When you pray, "Give to us," it's not a demanding or a commanding prayer. It is simply the acknowledgment that there's nothing the sovereign God can't do for us or won't give us if we ask. "Give" indicates our complete dependence on God for everything.

The next word in this phrase is *us*. It's important for us to remember that Jesus did not command us to pray, "Give *me*." No. That's a bad prayer. *"Give me this day."* No, no, no. Jesus made it abundantly clear that we should not only pray for ourselves, but we should pray for the needs of others also. We have siblings. Lord, give *us*—the whole household, the whole neighborhood, the whole congregation—give to *us*!

Now let's go to *this day*. "This day" reminds us not to get ahead of ourselves. It reminds us that our Christian walk is a *daily* walk, and we need a *daily* renewal of God's grace, God's mercy, and God's provision. When we pray, "Give us this day," it reminds us that Jesus wants us to live in the present.

> In Matthew 6—the same chapter where the model prayer is—Jesus said this: *"Take therefore no thought for the morrow: for the morrow shall take thought for the things of itself. Sufficient unto the day is the evil thereof"* (MATTHEW 6:34 KJV).

We can't be worried about tomorrow. You are worried about tomorrow when you aren't even sure about tonight. The way this is set up is that we don't know when we're going to heaven. Now, this does not speak against vision or against planning, but don't spend all of your time thinking about tomorrow. Live in today. Don't live in your past. Don't live in your future. Live in today. Enjoy the place where you are now. Enjoy the job you have now. Enjoy the people you are surrounded by now. Don't look back longingly to a place you were, or look desperately to a place that you hope to be someday. When we meditate on the past or the future, we miss out on what God wants to do in us, and through us, in the present.

So when we pray, "Give us this day," we are not simply asking for God's help, but we are putting our trust in God completely, knowing that the need we have this day will be met by Him *this day*. What we are, in fact, asking for is freedom from worry. We need freedom so that we're no longer grieving over past failures or anxious over things to come. He helps us there too.

> Let's take a look at Matthew 6 again: *"For after all these things the Gentiles seek. For your heavenly*

Father knows that you need all these things" (MATTHEW 6:32).

He knows what you need. So just ask Him.

"But seek first the kingdom of God and His righteousness, and all these things shall be added to you" (MATTHEW 6:33).

This text is telling us, "don't sweat it." God knows you need all of these things, including love. He has not forgotten you. God *so loved the world*. He loves. God is love. And God wants to give you love. He wants to make sure to give you somebody who will love you. He takes care of the fish of the sea, and the fowl of the air, and the beasts of the field and He will take care of you. And because these things are what we need, and because we can't do without certain things, what is appointed for us by God's providence is ours.

Now, during Bible times, bread was a main source of food in households and affordable to all families. It was a staple. Those of you who have traveled to Israel would know that at all the buffets, for lunch and dinner, they're going to serve a whole bunch of bread. That's a staple. Bread and wine are two of the greatest staples in Israel. And that's what we use for communion: bread and wine. Still to this day, bread and wine are staples in the Holy Land.

Bread is a symbol for all the material needs of life. In this model prayer, bread is symbolic of our daily needs. When Jesus told us to pray, "Give us this day our daily bread," He was not just talking about Wonder Bread, raisin bread, homemade bread, or St. Peter's bread; He wasn't talking about what you can consume in your mouth. No, no, no. In those days, bread carried with it the connotation of all of one's needs. He was saying, "When you pray, you must pray, 'Give us this day our daily needs.'"

Now, there are three categories of basic human needs. The first is physical—things like shelter, food, and clothing.

The second are emotional needs—things like stability, confidence, self-esteem, and even love. The third are spiritual needs to fulfill the longings of the soul. All of these are encapsulated in that word *bread*. So, when you pray, "Give us this day our daily bread," it is not limited to a Jehovah-Jireh moment.

Next, when we pray, "Give us this day our daily bread," we acknowledge and admit two things. First, we are saying that God provides what we really need. And second, God provides it when we need it the most. You have got to know that. You have got to be convinced of this—that first, God provides what we need, and that second, He provides it when we really need it. There is no way we will ever have a need, then go to God and ask for it, and He does not provide for it. Earthly fathers do better than that. How much more will our heavenly Father provide for us?

Now that you have a foundation for this particular phrase, I can answer the conundrum that I gave you at the beginning of this chapter. Look at these verses again:

> *"In the sweat of your face you shall eat bread till you return to the ground, for out of it you were taken; for dust you are, and to dust you shall return."*
>
> —GENESIS 3:19

> *"Man shall not live by bread alone, but by every word that proceeds from the mouth of God."*
>
> —MATTHEW 4:4

> *For even when we were with you, we commanded you this: If anyone will not work, neither shall he eat.*
>
> —2 THESSALONIANS 3:10

Now, looking at all of this, and keeping in the back of our minds that it was Jesus who said: "When you pray, ask the Lord to give you your daily bread," let's continue.

After the fall in the Garden of Eden, man was commanded to "earn his bread" by the "sweat of his brow." So, work is one of the ways that God has designed for us to receive His provision. So to say the words "give us" does not mean we are begging God for food. If we don't work, we shouldn't eat, Paul wrote. Translation: If you don't work, you shouldn't expect to be provided for. So, when we pray, "Give us this day our daily bread," what we are really praying is, "Lord, give us work."

You can't pray, "Give us this day our daily bread," and then just sit back and wait for God to throw food down on you. *Bread* is equivalent here in this context to *work*. And ladies and gentlemen, the privilege to work is a gift. The blessing to work or the power to work is a privilege. The love of work will bring success. If you don't like to work, you're lazy. And if you're lazy, you won't succeed. If you don't like to work and if you're lazy, just scratch this part of the prayer out! If you're retired after a lifetime of work, there's a system in place for that. You should have worked long enough that you have a pension. And you should also have children who can now help provide for you. This is how the system works: once a man, twice a child. When I was a child, my parents took care of me. When I became an adult, I took care of my children. When I move into old age, my children will take care of me. That's how it works. And that's why you see the words in scripture, "Honor your mother and your father." When they can no longer do for themselves, and you give to them of what you have, you honor them like they honored you while you were children.

Pray and ask the Lord to give you this day your daily supply of help. Every day, pray, "Keep me holy." Every day pray, "Keep me healthy."

So, when you pray, "Give us this day," you're praying, "Lord, You give us the power to get wealth, so give me power for this day. Give me the desire and the opportunity to work today."

Finally, let's look at Matthew 4:1–4:

Then was Jesus led up of the Spirit into the wilderness to be tempted of the devil. And when he had fasted forty days and forty nights, he was afterward an hungered. And when the tempter came to him, he said, If thou be the Son of God, command that these stones be made bread. But he answered and said, It is written, Man shall not live by bread alone, but by every word that proceedeth out of the mouth of God." (MATTHEW 4:1–4 KJV)

Go to God for your emotional needs. Go to God for your physical needs. But when you pray, "God, give us this day our daily bread," keep in mind that you can't live by that alone. Because if you have money, if you have a job, and if you have love, some of your needs are being met, but your soul is lost! You're an incomplete person.

The same Jesus who told you to pray for your daily bread is the same Jesus who said, "Man shall not live by bread alone, but by every word that proceeds from the mouth of God." That's why you go to church. You are looking for the proceeding word from God's mouth. Look for the word that builds on last week's word, that proceeds. As a pastor, I preach a lot of series, because man shall live by every word that *proceeds*. And as an author, I know that the power of a book allows you to set your eyes upon the Word daily!

So, as your soul is satisfied, when you pray, "Give us our daily bread," you're saying to God, "Give us the joy we need for today. Give us the grace we need for today. Give us the peace we need for today." It's pointless to have money and be without peace.

Begin to pray this prayer: "Lord, give me the peace I need today. Give me the righteousness I need today. Give me the composure I need today. Give me the character development I need today. Help me to represent You today in a way that would bring pleasure to You. Give me this day my daily bread."

The phrase, "Give us this day our daily bread," is not just a Jehovah-Jireh request for Him to meet our needs. No, bread represents everything. So, you need to know the names of God. When you pray, "Give us this day everything we need," make sure you are also hallowing His name, telling Him, "Master, You're the Master Creator! I need to get something started in my life. Be my Adonai today. Be my El Shaddai, my strong tower, because I'm anxious about something today, God. Be my El Elyon, my most High God. I need You to lift my spirit to a higher place, so that even though my body is here, my spirit is elevated above the nuisances of this day. Be my Elohim, my sovereign Ruler and God. Yes, be my Jehovah-Jireh, my Provider, but also be my Jehovah-Rapha, my Healer. And be my Jehovah-Shalom, my Peace. And be my Jehovah-Shammah, the God who is always there. And be my Jehovah-Nissi, the Lord my Banner. And be my Jehovah-Rohi, the Lord my Shepherd. Give me everything I need today—today!" This is the power under the heading in the model prayer, "Give us this day our daily bread."

Forgive Us as We Forgive Others

Forgive Us as We Forgive Others

THIS PETITION IS PERHAPS THE MOST challenging of the four petitions for most people. Listen to what Jesus asks: "When you pray, pray like this: Forgive us our trespasses, just like we forgive those who trespass against us."

I have one question: *Really?*

This prayer is saying to the Father, "However I choose to forgive other people, that's how I want You to forgive me." That is a bold request. And it should cause us all to take a step back to check our hearts and make sure that we do not have any unforgiveness or animosity toward others.

When you come to this point in the model prayer, you are asking God to forgive you of your trespasses, but you're also acknowledging that, like the rest of us, you have some sins in your life. You have fallen short of the glory of God. That's what you're acknowledging.

This prayer for forgiveness is the only petition in the entire model prayer that comes with a condition attached to it. If we do not forgive, Jesus tells us to pray, then Father, don't forgive us. And if we do forgive at all, then use the formula we use to forgive others to determine how You will forgive us.

Notice very carefully here that even though Jesus makes forgiveness a prerequisite for answered prayers—and we're going to see this even more clearly in a bit—this petition does *not* come first. We are not required to clear the air with the other person before we pray. "Get righteous, get holy, and confess your sins before you even call Me"—we're not required to do that. Instead, Jesus invites us to connect with His sovereignty, with His purpose, with His provision, and *then* to ask for forgiveness.

FORGIVE US AS WE FORGIVE OTHERS

I see in this petition a lot of grace. God doesn't withhold the kingdom from us until we forgive or are forgiven. Instead, He gives us the kingdom so that we can forgive and be forgiven. It doesn't say, "Until you forgive, forget the kingdom." God doesn't operate like that. And we all should praise the Lord for His grace!

In one of his books, Robert Louis Stevenson tells the story of two sisters who never married and lived together in the same house for years.

> *One day the two sisters fell out and decided never to speak to one another again. Two sisters. Blood. Siblings. Sisters. They fell out! They fell out with one another and decided, "I'm not talking to you ever again as long as I live!"*
>
> *So, with a piece of chalk, they divided up every area of their house in half. Chalk. They chalked it up! With a piece of chalk, they drew a line across the sofa. "This is your half. This is*

my half." With a piece of chalk, they drew a line right through the middle of the kitchen. "This is your half. This is my half." With a piece of chalk, the doorways were divided. "You go in on this side, and I go in and come out on this side." The two women lived the rest of their lives imprisoned in bitterness. Bitterness had them bound. They refused to even acknowledge each other's presence. In other words, no, "Good morning." No, "Good evening." No, "How are you doing?" No, "How was your day?"

Now, I know you may be thinking, "There is nothing strange about that. That's how our house is!" But with one piece of chalk, they marked each other completely out of their lives. And the story is they both died still chalked out.

Today, believe it or not, many people are behaving like this. "I don't want anything more to do with you. I'm drawing a chalk line, even though it may be imaginary." Most of us, at one point or another, have had someone with whom we've fallen out. Well, let me clear the air for you and help you out. All of us who are over the age of ten have fallen out with at least one person in our lives. There have been times when anger has filled our hearts, and we felt that we would never be able to forgive or forget that person or what they did. This is a dangerous place to get to in your life. And it is an even more dangerous place to get stuck in.

Unresolved conflict is more dangerous than you may wish to realize. It is known to bring about chronic stress, depression, and even paranoid personality disorder. Oftentimes people will hate you, but it has nothing to do with you and everything to do with themselves. They will hate you because they hate themselves. They may also not have a problem with you at all, but they are just habitually living in unforgiveness.

It has been proven that patients suffering from depression due to unforgiveness have little or no self-control. This limits their ability to maintain proper social functionality. Unforgiveness can have a direct impact on the mental health and psychology of a person, and if it is not treated, it can eventually lead to suicidal tendencies. Noted psychiatrists have indicated that when treating mentally ill or disturbed patients, the act of forgiveness often facilitates the process of recovery from mental trauma.

Unforgiveness in our heart can take the form of a list... Do you keep a list of the people who've hurt you or mistreated you? Do you have a list? It could be written or unwritten. Keeping a mental list of offenders sends a strong message to yourself that you've not yet forgiven them. You still have a strong desire to get back at them. You probably, somehow, want to make them experience the same degree of pain they caused you.

Forgiveness means different things to different people. Generally, however, forgiveness is the process whereby someone who has been wronged chooses to let go of their resentment and thoughts of revenge and instead treat the wrongdoer with compassion. Wow! That is forgiveness. Forgiveness does not mean forgetting or excusing the harm that was done to you, or even necessarily making up with the person who caused you the harm. Forgiveness, though, can lessen the grip that resentment has on you and help free you from the control of the person who harmed you. The truth is, you will have difficulty making things right with God until you make it right with those persons who have hurt you and done you wrong.

Jesus instructs us to pray, "Forgive us our trespasses, as we forgive those who trespass against us." Somehow, we've got to find the strength to be able to forgive—and even to forgive ex-husbands and ex-wives, to forgive old boyfriends and old girlfriends, to forgive your children's father, the man who didn't marry you. You've got to find the strength to forgive the people who betrayed you, the people who backstabbed you, the people who denied you, the supervisor who blocked your promotion.

You've got to find a way. You've got to find the strength to forgive them and let it go. Let me tell you why. If you fail to forgive them, that person whom you consider to be your enemy will direct your life via remote control. They can stay right where they are and determine which channel you live the rest of your life on because unforgiveness binds you to them.

You cannot get ahead in your life while you're trying to get even with your enemy. It can't happen. You can only do one thing at a time. If you are trying to get even with your enemy, you will give that everything you've got. But while you're doing that, make sure you understand that you're getting further and further away from your life's goal. So, you can have one or the other. You may gain the satisfaction of seeing your enemy hurt, or you can continue to make progress in your life and decide for yourself which channel you want to live on.

I know you're anointed, and you have a strong prayer life, but for this particular petition, you need more than God's anointing to accomplish it. You need a made-up mind, the understanding that you *have* to do this.

Forgiveness is an attribute of the strong. Unforgiveness is evidence of weakness. It takes strength to speak from your heart and not just with your mouth. When you forgive, you do it from a position of strength and power. I have decided I'm not going to let anyone run my life via remote control. Now, don't get me wrong: When you forgive from the heart, it doesn't necessarily mean that you will have corresponding *feelings*. You may still *feel* some anger toward that person. You may still *feel* hurt and betrayed by that person. You may still *feel* as if that person hasn't made any changes or an effort to make things right. And yet, forgiving someone from your heart involves making the quality decision to let all of that go. You may have feelings that rise up when you see them, but you must quell those feelings with acts of kindness and thoughts of God's words.

You have to fight unforgiveness like you would anything else. But it's the strong who overcome, who endure until the end. Eventually, your emotions will catch up with your faith, your choices, and your actions, and then you will only harbor love for that individual who did you wrong. It may seem inconceivable, or even impossible, but with God, you can walk in complete forgiveness in your life.

There's a place that God has prepared for each of us. It's a place of blessing, a place of refreshing, a place of fulfillment. But if you want to get to that place, you must develop and maintain the capacity to forgive. The mentality that says, "I'll get him back if that's the last thing I do!" will hold you back. You can't let go with that mentality because that's all you will ever do in your life. You'll miss your destiny, convicted of the fact that you will get him if that's the last thing you do.

You can't make that statement with conviction and also serve God. When you make statements like those, you rip any love you have left right out of your heart.

As people of God, as prayed-up believers, our tomorrows must include a world in which forgiveness is practiced and reconciliation is embraced.

Don't look to global and national leaders to practice this. They will not set a good example in this regard. Most politicians, in particular, have one goal primarily, and that is to win! They'll bruise up whomever they have to and do so without apology. So, in order to forgive, you have got to let go of resentment, and you have to let go of your list of enemies.

> *Beloved, do not avenge yourselves, but rather give place to wrath; for it is written, "Vengeance is Mine, I will repay," says the Lord.*
>
> —ROMANS 12:19

"Vengeance is Mine," God says! He will repay them. You've got to give up the privilege of doing it yourself! And it is a privilege. Long ago I gave up my "privilege" to retaliate against others. I'm a Christian! That means that when I said yes to Jesus, and when I pray this prayer, "Forgive us our trespasses," I am giving up the privilege I had of seeking revenge. I am really giving up the privilege of nursing a grudge. There is a big difference between nursing a grudge and trying to get rid of a grudge. When you nurse a grudge, you are feeding it. You are indulging in it. You are giving attention to those feelings of hatred and betrayal. It's a matter of the heart and a matter of the mind. The difference is that you behave kindly toward someone in public but go home and secretly wish that they would get what's coming to them for their negative behavior. You *personally* are not trying to get even. You *personally* are not contributing to their misfortune, but you *are* harboring and nursing a grudge. A lot of other people can't even tell, because you are keeping quiet, but both you and God know that your heart is acting in a completely different fashion and that you are living in hypocrisy. This is what nursing a grudge is like. But let's take a step back and talk about what a grudge is in the first place.

A *grudge* is a deep, ongoing resentment that you cultivate in your heart against someone. A grudge is an unforgiving spirit that leads to unforgiving attitudes and unforgiving actions. Harboring a grudge is about nursing a dislike for someone else. Grudges are dangerous because they are destructive. Grudges that are filled with resentment, vengeance, and hostility can take deep root in your life and in your spirit. Grudges have destroyed marriages. Grudges have broken up families. Grudges have ruined relationships. Grudges have split churches. Grudges are not only destructive, but they are also *self*-destructive. When you hold a grudge against someone, you will hurt yourself as much and perhaps more than you will hurt the person against whom you are holding the grudge.

Letting go of grudges can lead to several things, including healthier relationships in your life. When you let your grudges go, you can have a healthier home. Letting them go brings improved mental health. Believe it or not, letting grudges go helps you physically too! It is known that when you let go of a grudge you lower your blood pressure... That could be the cause of many people's chronic high blood pressure. It may not be the steak. It may not be the red meat. It may be a grudge! It can kill you!

> *"Moreover if your brother sins against you, go and tell him his fault between you and him alone. If he hears you, you have gained your brother. But if he will not hear, take with you one or two more, that 'by the mouth of two or three witnesses every word may be established.' And if he refuses to hear them, tell it to the church.*

FORGIVE US AS WE FORGIVE OTHERS

But if he refuses even to hear the church, let him be to you like a heathen and a tax collector."

—MATTHEW 18:15–17

Mark them! Ignore them. Don't use them. This is Jesus talking here. Go to the church, and if they still come before the church and say, "Listen, man, I am not for him," then Jesus says to not use them. Treat them like a heathen.

Many churches are bound up because they simply don't follow the Scriptures. They let heathens dictate the temperature of their assembly. Unsaved heathens, living all kinds of bad lives, who would never confess and ask God for a pardon, who wouldn't pardon their brother, are directing the choir. They are overseeing the usher board. They are running up and down the church like demons on parade. It is time for the body of Christ to wake up to what is happening!

There is another word for the act of unforgiveness besides *grudge*. It is a word that many have not associated with unforgiveness: *judgment*.

> *"For in the same way you judge others, you will be judged, and with the measure you use, it will be measured to you."*
>
> —MATTHEW 7:2 NIV

So many people have stood on this audacious throne of superiority and cast judgment on others for what they have done. You are not their God, nor are you in a position to cast judgment on anyone else. The matter is between them and God! *Stop judging!* Church people are too judgmental. Stop judging, because the same way you judge others, that's how God will judge you. Is that what you want? Do you want God to dispense with His grace in your life and judge you the way you're judging other people?

The body of Christ would be stronger, more powerful, and more influential if the judgment of others would stop now! I'm not talking specifically; I'm talking generically. But many of us in the body of Christ have delved too much into other people's business. And here is the problem. You are trying to take the place of God in other people's lives. How arrogant and prideful can you be? You are not God! You have no right to judge. There is only one Judge, and He has not abdicated His throne. Who would dare try to sit on it and pass decrees in His stead?

We should all be so very careful when it comes to the area of unforgiveness and judgment. When in doubt, forgive, give grace, and offer mercy.

> *"And when you stand praying, if you hold anything against anyone, forgive them, so that your Father in heaven may forgive you your sins."*
>
> —MARK 11:25 NIV

Do you know why some of your prayers aren't getting through? Could the reason be that you are continuing to harbor things in your heart? This is why forgiveness is a topic in the model prayer. God wants to answer your prayers—and in order to do that, He needs to forgive you—and in order for that to happen, you have to ask Him for forgiveness—and for Him to follow through on that request, He checks your heart to see if you are free of bitterness, resentment, judgment, and unforgiveness. Only then is He able to liberally lather on His forgiveness, mercy, and grace in your life.

> *Bear with each other and forgive one another if any of you has a grievance against someone. Forgive as the Lord forgave you.*
>
> —COLOSSIANS 3:13 NIV

That means we must be patient. Jesus helps us bear with each other. You don't know the hell some people are going through when you walk up and talk to them. Judging people for what they are doing, and where they're at, is incredibly foolish, because you have no way of knowing what is going on inside their hearts. Somebody could have just gotten saved, then walks into the church cussing and looking disreputable; instead of judging them, we should flock to that person and rejoice with them that they have found God! Don't be so quick to judge, but instead be ready to supply grace and give mercy. Bear with one another and forgive whatever grievances you have against one another. For Christians, walking in unforgiveness is not an option. You are a Christian because you've been forgiven. Jesus tells you to forgive others just like God has forgiven you.

Lewis Smedes once said, *"To forgive is to set a prisoner free, only to discover most times that that prisoner was you."*[1]

Free yourself up! You have to free yourself! It is a choice that you make. God doesn't make it for you. You can't pray, "Lord, free me of this unforgiveness." No. That is not how it works. God is not going to do for you what He has told you to do yourself. That's *your* decision. You have to *choose* to be free. It is a personal choice. You can choose to live in freedom and walk in victory, or you can choose to live in bondage. It's a choice.

When I choose to ask God to forgive me, He will. But He will not help me to forgive others. We must pray, "Forgive us, as we..." It's a prerequisite. It has a condition attached to it. If you cannot forgive other people, more than likely you are living with heavy unforgiveness in your heart.

I've forgiven colleagues who hurt me. I have forgiven bishops who stabbed me in the back. I have forgiven church members who have abused my kindness. I have forgiven people who have talked badly about me, maligned my character, and tried to destroy my name without having ever met me. The only thing they know of me is what they were told. They don't know me personally. But, I have chosen to forgive them.

I cannot afford to come up to the pulpit still wounded. Wounded people wound other people. Instead, I come with the intention to preach from a perspective of victory and deliverance and progress and faith, and yes, God is able! That's my perspective! And you've

FORGIVE US AS WE FORGIVE OTHERS

got to decide to live like that. It is not automatic because you know Jesus. Ultimately, our willingness to forgive has to be based upon what God has done *for* us, not what people have done *to* us.

I'm sure you could look back in your life and find at least one scenario that, when you share it with your brother or sister, you would feel justified in your unforgiveness. But this ought not be! We as Christians have to learn to walk in love and compassion for others without using pity and judgment to back up our claims of offense! Walking in forgiveness and grace should not lead us into being insensitive.

What the other person did to you may have been wrong. The way they handled you was wrong. The way they treated your children because of the animosity that exists between you two was wrong. But your willingness to forgive must be based upon what God has done for you, and not what people have done to you. As a believer, you should not instantly turn your hurting brothers and sisters away, declaring that they just need to forgive and forget. You should bear with other's hurts and love on them. Cook them up something warm, give them a change of clothes, let them rest on your couch. If they want to talk bad about someone else, you don't have to join in, but you can still have compassion for them, that they had to go through a difficult experience.

I believe with all my heart that if I had harbored malice, envy, or grudges toward the people who perpetrated evil against me in my past, then the church that I pastor now, as well as my personal life, would not be where it is today. But because I let it go and let God have His way, He has done and continues to do amazing things in my life. When you leave it to God, He blesses the work of your hands.

So, how often are we to offer forgiveness to another person?

Then Peter came to Jesus and asked, "Lord, how many times

shall I forgive my brother or sister who sins against me? Up to seven times?" Jesus answered, "I tell you, not seven times, but seventy-seven times."

—Matthew 18:21–22 NIV

That's four hundred and ninety times! Jesus wasn't talking about a specific number though. He was using a euphemism. He was saying, "Listen, man. You should keep on forgiving, not for just their sake, but for your sake." And in this area of repeated offense, there is one aspect of forgiveness and walking in love that is essential. It is the difference between love and trust. I can love you, but not trust you. I could wish nothing but the best for you, I could harbor no ill will toward you, but I could still not trust you with my family, my money, or my vocation. Love is given freely, trust is earned. Forgiveness will always be available, but trust, once severed, can take years to rebuild. When somebody treats you wrong, if they mishandle your money and mistreat you and your family, love forgives them for what they have done. Nothing that another person does should ever make you hate them. You may hate what they did, but you should not hate the person. However, people *can* do things that betray your trust, and you are not obligated to place your trust in them again.

There is a difference between forgiving someone and trusting them again. If somebody steals from you after you trusted them with your money, forgiveness does not dictate that you must trust them again with more money. I know this seems like common sense, but many people have blurred the lines in this area. Forgiveness wipes the slate clean between you two, but if the other person is going to want to be trusted again, then he or she will have to earn that trust back over the course of time. We have to exercise wisdom in these areas.

Finally, forgiveness initiates the process. You have more than likely heard it said, or maybe you've said it yourself,

"I'll forgive them when they say they are sorry." Oops. You are forgiving the way the world forgives... Waiting for them to apologize first is not God's way. You cannot wait for somebody to say, "I apologize. I'm so sorry." You've got to go ahead of them and forgive them.

God **did not** tell you to forgive others when they apologize.

God **did not** say, "Forgive others whenever you can really tell that they feel bad for what they have done."

God **did not** say, "Forgive others whenever they make an effort to correct what they messed up."

That is how the world does it! Worldly people are kind to those who are kind to them. They are generous with those who are generous to them. They love those who love them in return... This is not the Christian way!

Jesus has something to say about this very topic in Luke 6. This is printed in red letters, a message from the Master Himself:

"But to you who are listening I say: Love your enemies, do good to those who hate you, bless those who curse you, pray for those who mistreat you. If someone slaps you on one cheek, turn to them the other also. If someone takes your coat, do not withhold your shirt from them. Give to everyone who asks you, and if anyone takes what belongs to you, do not demand it back. Do to others as you would have them do to you. If you love those who love you, what credit is that to you? Even sinners love those who love them. And if you do good to those who are good to you, what credit is that to you? Even sinners do that. And if you lend to those from whom you expect repayment, what credit is that to you? Even sinners lend to sinners, expecting to be repaid in full. But love your enemies, do good to them, and lend to them without expecting

FORGIVE US AS WE FORGIVE OTHERS

to get anything back. Then your reward will be great, and you will be children of the Most High, because he is kind to the ungrateful and wicked. Be merciful, just as your Father is merciful. Do not judge, and you will not be judged. Do not condemn, and you will not be condemned. Forgive, and you will be forgiven. Give, and it will be given to you. A good measure, pressed down, shaken together and running over, will be poured into your lap. For with the measure you use, it will be measured to you."

—LUKE 6:27-38 NIV

This is the attitude of forgiveness that we should carry around with us! The miracle of forgiveness is the creation of a new beginning. It does not always take away the hurt. It does not deny the past injury that was caused. It merely refuses to let these things stand in the way of a new start for you. Anger, bitterness, malice, and unforgiveness are all spiritual poisons for which forgiveness is the only cure! Follow these words of Jesus and watch as the spirit of freedom begins to manifest in your life!

Endnotes

[1] Lewis B. Smedes, *Forgive and Forget: Healing the Hurts We Don't Deserve.*

About The Author

Bishop Neil C. Ellis is the presiding prelate of the Global United Fellowship (GUF), with more than 1,400 churches in 42 countries. GUF serves as an international body of spiritual leaders, fellowships, and congregations united to strategically plan, implement, and execute transformative and generational change.

Bishop Ellis is the senior pastor of Mount Tabor Church in Nassau, Bahamas. This church has grown from 11 charter members in 1987 to thousands of members and thousands more who are a part of the Internet Church, Mount Tabor Anytime. As a pastor to pastors, he mentors a large number of pastors around The Bahamas, Europe, and the United States and serves as a counselor and advisor to hundreds of pastors around the world.

Bishop Ellis has been recognized by Her Majesty, Queen Elizabeth of England for rendering distinguished services in Commonwealth nations and is also the recipient of the 2010 Trumpet Award for Spiritual Enlightenment. He is the youngest living inductee in the International Civil Rights Walk of Fame located in Atlanta, Georgia. He is also the author of several books and is a much sought after conference speaker and prophetic teacher.

Bishop Ellis and his wife reside in Nassau, Bahamas along with their two children.